Penguin Readers

BOYS DON'T CRY

MALORIE BLACKMAN

RETOLD BY MAEVE CLARKE
ILLUSTRATED BY ANA LATESE
SERIES EDITOR: SORREL PITTS

Contents

Parts of this story are told by a 17-year-old boy called Dante.

And parts of it are told by his younger brother, Adam.

Look for their names, DANTE and ADAM, to see who is telling the next part of the story.

Chapter One

Results day

DANTE

Good luck today. Hope that you get what you want and need. :)

I smiled at the text from my girlfriend, Collette – but not for long. I was too nervous. Today was A level exam results day! I only needed four good A levels and then I couldgo to university – a year earlier than all my friends.

My A levels were my chance for a better life, and then *after* university when I had a good job, things would be different. And my family wouldn't need to worry about money in the same way.

Where was the postman? My whole future was

in his postbag. It was strange how one piece of paper was going to change the rest of my life.

Just then the doorbell rang, and I ran to the front door.

It wasn't the postman.

It was Melanie – and she wasn't alone. There was a baby in a buggy next to her.

"Hello, Dante," she said. "C– can I come in?"

"Er – yeah. Of course."

She went into the sitting room and I followed. What did she want?

"Are you babysitting?" I pointed to the baby.

"That's one way to describe it," Melanie replied as she looked around the room at the family photos. Some were of me, more were of Adam, but most were of Mum. Dad used to take lots of photos, but after Mum died, he hadn't used his camera again.

Melanie looked the same as ever, maybe a little slimmer, but that was all. She was wearing black jeans and a dark blue jacket over a light blue T-shirt. Her dark brown hair was shorter than before, but she was still beautiful. And she had the biggest brown eyes I had ever seen.

"What's its name?" I asked.

"*Her* name is Emma," she said. "Do you want to hold her?"

"Er . . . no thank you."

Was Melanie mad? Of course I didn't want to hold a baby. Why was she here? Where had she been since she stopped coming to school over eighteen months ago?

"I went to live with my aunt," Melanie said, as if reading my mind. "I'm back for the day and I was close, so I thought that I'd come and say 'hi'. I hope you don't mind."

I shook my head and gave a little smile.

"I'm going away today actually," Melanie continued, "to stay with some friends who live in the north."

"So what have you been doing?" I asked. I couldn't think of anything else to say.

"I've been looking after Emma."

"Yes, but what else have you been doing?"

Melanie gave a small smile but didn't reply, and I was glad when the baby started to make baby noises and broke the silence.

"What are your plans now you've finished your A levels?" Melanie asked, picking the baby up.

She looked at me properly for the first time and I noticed that her eyes seemed . . . older and sadder than I remembered.

"If I've passed, I'm going to study history at university and then become a journalist after that. I want to write about wars and politics –

important things." After a pause I asked, "Whose baby is she? Is she a relative?"

Just at that moment, the baby started to cry very softly, but it sounded like the start of a bigger, longer cry.

"Her nappy needs changing. Hold her for a moment." Melanie pushed the baby at me, so I had to take it – but I held it away from me. She opened the large blue baby bag hanging on the back of the buggy and took out a yellow, plastic baby mat which she put on the carpet. She also took out a nappy, some baby wipes, and a small orange plastic bag.

She laid the baby on the plastic mat and took off its yellow babygro. Suddenly she started saying silly things like, "Am I going to change your nappy now? Yes, I am. Oh yes, I am." When she undid the nappy, it was completely full of smelly baby poo. I wanted to be sick.

"You should watch this," Melanie said. "You might learn something."

"Yes, but why would I want to?"

Melanie cleaned the baby's bottom, put the dirty nappy in the plastic orange bag and then held it out to me. "Can you put this in the bin please?"

I carefully held the plastic bag away from me and ran to the kitchen, where I threw it in the bin. Melanie watched me return with a smile in her eyes.

"Mel," I began. "Why . . .?"

"Shush," she whispered, putting the baby back in the buggy. "She's fallen asleep." Then suddenly, she pulled a piece of paper from her bag.

"Read this," she said.

I opened the document. It was a birth certificate.

I stared at her. "You're the baby's mother?"

"Dante," she said, "I need to tell you something . . ."

Mel was only 18. Had she never heard of the pill?

She took a deep breath, "Dante, you're the dad. Emma is our daughter."

Melanie's words hit me like a punch between the eyes and I felt so sick, I had to sit down. I couldn't speak. And I couldn't think.

How could this be true?

But now I was starting to remember things that I didn't want to – like the Christmas party at Rick's house almost two years ago.

Remembering that night was like looking at a series of photographs, and as the night got later, the photos became less and less clear. Melanie and I had only been going out for a couple of months at the time. At the party, we danced and drank and kissed, and then drank and danced and kissed some more. Somebody shouted, "Get a room!"

So just for fun, we went upstairs and into the first room we saw. We closed the door and started kissing again.

It had been the first time – for both of us.

It was the one and only time and to be honest – it finished very, very quickly.

I remember thinking, *Is that it?*

Now that *one* little moment had turned into this.

"I don't believe you," I said. "My name's not even on the birth certificate. How can you be sure the baby's mine?"

Chapter Two

Headaches

ADAM

"Another headache, Adam?" Dad looked at me as I sat at the kitchen table.

I nodded as I gently moved my fingers along the sides of my head. For the past couple of weeks, I'd had some really bad headaches.

"Take something for the pain?" my brother Dante said.

"You know I don't believe that it's good to take pills," I told him.

"But you've got a headache," Dante argued.

"I'm not taking any pills."

"Time for you to go to the doctor's," Dad said. "You've been having too many headaches."

"It's the heat," I replied. "I just need to lie

down for a while." The only word I hated more than "doctor" was "hospital". Just thinking about it was making me hot and uncomfortable.

"You've been having headaches since the match against Colliers Green School," said Dante. "Are you sure you're . . .?"

"Stop talking about it!"

"What match?" asked Dad.

"The ball hit Adam on the head," said Dante. "Luckily his head is totally empty, so no damage was done."

"Adam, you never told me that," Dad said.

"Dad, it's just a headache." And now my dad and brother were making it worse.

"Put your shoes on, Adam," Dad said. "I'm taking you to the doctor's."

So here I was with Dad, on my way to the doctor's. There was nothing that I could do.

Chapter Three

Boys don't cry

DANTE

"I've never been with anyone except you, Dante!" Melanie's voice was pure ice. "Don't you ever say that again. I couldn't put your name on the birth certificate because we're not married and you weren't there with me." She looked at me angrily. "Anyway, I didn't come here to argue with you."

"Then why did you come?" I asked. "Why didn't you have an abortion, or think about adoption?"

"I thought about it," she said with tears in her eyes, "but from the moment that I found I was pregnant – Emma was real to me. Do you know my mum made me leave home for getting pregnant?"

"What?"

"My aunt let me stay with her, but only until the baby was born. After that, she wanted another family to adopt the baby. But I couldn't do it."

"Why didn't you tell me?"

"You couldn't help," she said with a small smile.

She was right. I couldn't help her.

Melanie looked at her watch. "I need to go to the shops and get some things for Emma. Could you look after her for a while?"

"No! Take *it* with you."

"Her name's Emma. And I'll be back in fifteen minutes or less. Please."

"No! You can't just leave your baby here."

Melanie was now at the front door. "Remember, she's your baby, too." She looked like she was going to cry.

"I'll be back soon."

And then she walked away without looking back.

What was I going to do?

What was Dad going to say?

———

When the doorbell rang, I jumped to my feet. Finally! Melanie had come back.

But it wasn't Melanie. It was the postman. He

15

handed me some letters. The top one was for me. I opened the envelope quickly – it was my exam results.

I had four A-stars.

In the sitting room, the baby started to cry. I wanted to cry, too, but I couldn't.

Boys don't cry – that's what Dad always said. And crying wouldn't help me now. All I could do was wait.

I sat in the armchair opposite the buggy and watched the baby cry. It cried and cried and then cried some more. Two minutes turned into five and five minutes turned into ten, and the baby was still crying. Finally, my phone rang – caller unknown.

"It's me. Melanie."

"Where the hell are you? It's been over an hour."

"I'm sorry, but I'm not coming back."

"What do you mean?"

"I'm not managing, Dante," she said. "I've tried and tried, but I can't. I need time to think. It'll be better for Emma to stay with you – you're her dad."

"You can't do this," I said. "You're just having a bad day."

"A bad day?" Melanie was going to cry at any moment. "I hate leaving Emma, but I don't have any other options."

"What are you talking about? It's your daughter."

"She's your daughter, too."

"But you're its mum."

"And you're her dad," she shot back. "What do I know about bringing up a kid? My dad left our family and my mum had two jobs just to put food on the table. I want something better for Emma. And if she stays with me, I'm afraid . . ."

"Afraid of what?"

"Dante, I love Emma and I'd die for her," Melanie's voice was little more than a whisper. "But sometimes when I'm alone and she won't stop crying . . . sometimes – the things I do . . . the things I want to do – scare me. Emma should be with someone who can really look after her."

"That's not me," I said, not really listening to what she was saying. "I don't know anything about babies."

"You'll learn. And you've got your dad and your brother and a big house."

"Mel. Don't do this!"

"I'm sorry, Dante. Tell Emma . . . tell her I love her."

Then she ended the call. I immediately tried to call her back, but my call went straight to voicemail. Had she blocked my number? I stared at my phone.

It took a few moments to realize that I was shaking – actually shaking. Melanie was free and I was not.

But I was going to university in less than a month and Melanie and her baby weren't going to stop me!

The thing was screaming up at me so loudly that I couldn't think, so I pushed the buggy up to the window. Maybe if it looked outside, it would see something interesting and stop crying. Then I went to the kitchen and called Collette. She was unhappy that I was asking about my last girlfriend. And she didn't have Melanie's latest mobile phone number or Melanie's aunt's mobile number or address either.

Now what was I going to do?

"Did you get your exam results?" Collette asked.

"Yeah, four A-stars," I said, quickly.

"That's fantastic," she said.

"Thanks."

"Well?" she said.

"What?"

"Aren't you going to ask about my results?" She sounded a little angry.

"Yes, I was just going to. Did you get the results

you wanted?"

"Yep, three A-stars and an A," Collette said, happily. "And we'll be at the same university – I can't wait," she said. "And tomorrow night we can celebrate at Bar Belle."

I didn't have time for this conversation. Dad and Adam would be back soon. "That's the doorbell," I lied. "I've got to go." Then I ended the call before she could say another word.

I spent the next twenty minutes calling everybody who might know where Melanie was, but nobody did. And all the time, the baby cried louder and louder without stopping.

In the end, I ran upstairs to my bedroom and waited . . . for an idea . . . for Mel to return . . . for this bad dream to end . . . for the sound of Dad's key in the lock.

Chapter Four

It's just a blood test

ADAM

"I'm not going, Dad."

"It's just a blood test and a scan at the hospital. That's all."

"I'm not going."

Dad gave a long sigh, but I meant what I said. If Dad thought that I didn't remember what had happened to Mum in hospital, he was wrong. I hated hospitals.

I'd watched my mum slowly die of cancer in one of them. She'd wanted to come home, but the doctors didn't let her.

I wasn't going to argue with Dad – anyway, I would have to wait weeks for a scan and my headaches would probably stop in a few days.

When we got home, I looked at our house for a moment before going inside. Our house was special in a way that other people didn't see. Sometimes, when I was at home alone or in a room by myself, I could *almost* hear Mum or smell her perfume or hear her laughter.

That's why I loved our house and I never wanted to live anywhere else.

Chapter Five

She's not coming back

DANTE

I sat down at the top of the stairs. My heart sounded loud in my chest. Dad and Adam looked up at me, waiting for me to speak.

"How did you do?" Adam asked, impatiently.

"I got four A-stars."

"I knew it," Adam said with a big smile on his face.

"So you passed, did you?" said Dad. "Good for you."

I tried not to feel sad. Why wasn't Dad proud that

I'd passed my A levels at 17 years of age instead of 18, like most other kids?

"So you'll be going to university?" said Dad.

"That's the plan," I replied, trying not to look

in the direction of the sitting room. Why couldn't Dad be a little more excited for me?

"Yes! Then I can have your bedroom!" Adam punched the air, then immediately held his head in pain.

"What did the doctor say?" I asked.

Adam stopped smiling. "She wants me to go to the hospital for some tests."

"Why? What's wrong with you?"

"Nothing – only that you're my brother."

Suddenly a noise came from the sitting room. It was obvious what was making it. I walked downstairs slowly as Dad moved into the sitting room, closely followed by Adam.

"Dante, why is there a baby in here?" Dad turned to look at me.

"It's . . . Do you remember Melanie Dyson? She brought it here earlier this morning. The baby's name is Emma. Emma Dyson."

"Melanie is here?" asked Dad.

"Ooh! Dante's upstairs with a girlfriend," Adam laughed.

"She's not my girlfriend. And she's not upstairs. She said that she was going to buy some things for the baby," I replied, "but she . . . she's not coming back."

"What?" Dad said. "Why would she leave her little sister here?"

"It's not her sister." I took a deep breath. "It's her daughter."

"Her daughter? Why would she . . .?" Dad looked at me hard and then turned to Adam.

"Adam," he said. "Go upstairs to your room."

"And do what?" Adam asked.

"I don't know. Find something to do," Dad shouted. "And shut the door behind you."

Chapter Six

Listen and learn

ADAM

Dad doesn't often shout at me, so I knew it was serious. Dad and Dante were watching each other.

I left the room, but I didn't close the door completely. Then I started to walk upstairs. I walked up the first two steps very noisily, waited for a moment and then quietly came back downstairs. I put my ear against the door and waited.

I had to know what was happening.

Chapter Seven

Holding the baby

DANTE

I didn't know what Dad was thinking as he looked down at the crying baby. Almost as soon as he picked it up, it laid its head on his shoulder and stopped crying.

"Why did Melanie leave her baby here?" he asked me slowly.

I kept my eyes on the carpet as I spoke. "She said – she's not managing . . . and . . . and she said that I'm the dad."

There was a long, long silence until I raised my head. Dad was staring at me with his mouth wide open.

"This is your daughter?"

"I don't know . . . Yes." My voice was very quiet.

"You stupid, bloody idiot," Dad said. His voice was too soft, too quiet. "You stupid . . ." He couldn't even look at me. "How could you be so stupid?" Now there was fire in his voice. "I never worried about you – your mum always said that Adam was the dreamer and that your head was in the right place. I'm glad your mum isn't alive to see this."

His last sentence cut me more deeply than anything else he'd said.

"I don't know what to say," Dad began. "I wanted you to become somebody, not have a kid at 17." He looked down at Emma. "So her mum has left you holding the baby?"

He gave a hard smile. "Have you held your daughter yet?"

Scared that I was going to drop it, I took it from Dad and brought it closer to my chest until its soft, smooth cheek was against my shoulder. It smelled of baby cream and milk.

Its body was warm against mine and its hair was soft against my neck.

And I hated it.

Dad sat on the sofa. "Now tell me everything, *everything* that happened this morning."

————

When I finished talking, he shook his head again. He was more than angry – the angrier he

27

was, the quieter he got.

"Were you and Melanie sleeping together often?"

My face began to burn. This wasn't the kind of conversation I wanted to have with my father.

"No. It was at Rick's party. And we'd both been drinking."

"So you weren't too drunk to have sex, just too drunk to use a condom."

"I've only had sex once, and that was with Melanie," I said again.

"Once is enough," said Dad. "Don't you know how babies are made?"

"Yes, Dad – but . . . I thought that Mel must be on the pill or something like that."

"It takes two to make a baby, Dante!"

"What am I going to do, Dad?" My voice shook as I spoke. "How can I look after a baby, if I'm going to university in a few weeks? Maybe someone can adopt or foster it."

As soon as I spoke, I knew that I'd made a mistake in saying the words aloud.

"You'd give away your own baby because this isn't a good moment for you?" asked Dad. "Adoption means you'd lose your own daughter forever. Is that what you really want?"

Yes! I'm 17 years old.

I felt guilty, but the kid in my arms was like a

wall between me and the rest of my life.

"Your daughter can't be adopted or fostered unless Melanie agrees – and you don't know where she is. So, you don't have many options," Dad said, slowly.

"Dad, I have no money, no job and I've only just got my A level results. What can I give a baby?"

"The same thing that I gave you and your brother. A roof over your head, food on the table and being there for you both. That's more important than you can imagine."

But I didn't really hear him. And he wasn't listening to me.

"So will you look after the baby while I go to university?" I asked.

Dad gave an ugly laugh. "How can I work full-time and look after *your* daughter at the same time?"

"How can I go to university and look after a baby at the same time?"

"You can't," said Dad.

"Well, what do I do now?"

"Grow up! Emma's yours for the next eighteen years. Get a job and look after your family!"

Family? Dad and Adam were my family. I didn't want or need anybody else. This baby would never belong here.

I wanted to punch the walls until blood came from my hands.

"Look at your daughter!" Dad said.

It was the first time that I looked at it properly. It had black hair and its face was round, with fat cheeks, smooth skin and a little pink mouth. Such a lot of noise could come from that mouth.

Did Dad think that I'd suddenly realize just how much I loved it? Well, I did not.

I felt nothing.

And that scared me more than anything else.

Chapter Eight

OMG

ADAM

Oh. My. God!

Dante has a kid?

Someone's coming. I'll have to go – just for now.

Chapter Nine

It's sleeping in my room?

DANTE

Dad took the day off work so that he could help me to get things ready.

"Thanks!" I said. It was just one word, but I really meant it.

Dad opened the large baby bag left by Melanie, and took out special baby milk, a baby bottle, some nappies, a book, an envelope full of papers, a babygro, a feeding cup and some baby food.

"These look like medical notes," he said when he opened the envelope. He put the papers back. "They can wait. There are more important things to think about. First of all, Emma needs food and a cot to sleep in."

I looked around the sitting room. "A cot's going to look a little silly in here."

"I agree," Dad said. "That's why it'll be at the end of your bed."

"What? No . . ."

"Where else is it going to go?"

"It's sleeping in my room?"

"Of course! Where else would she sleep? And calling Emma 'it' isn't going to change a thing. Now, I'm going to buy some things for Emma. I'll be back soon."

As soon as Dad left the room, I heard him talking to my brother. "Adam! When I'm having a private conversation, don't listen at the bloody door."

My brother always wanted to know everything, and the moment Dad left the house, Adam came in.

"Oh my God! You've got a daughter?" Adam's eyes were as round and as bright as a full moon.

"This is Emma."

"Can I hold her?" he asked, sitting down and holding out his hands. "I won't drop her. I promise."

He held the baby safe in his arms and kissed its head. "Hello, Emma," he said, softly. "Aren't you beautiful? I'm your Uncle Adam."

My brother was only 16 years old and he was already an uncle. Adam looked so happy – it was clear in his face, his whole body. The baby

33

opened its eyes. Oh no! I waited for the noise to begin, but the baby looked at my brother, smiled and went straight back to sleep.

"I'm your Uncle Adam and I love you."

I'd never heard Adam say he loved anyone, but just like that he loved the baby. How did that work? And why did it make me feel so empty?

Chapter Ten

Just a phase

DANTE

While Adam looked after Emma, I went online to find out about DNA tests. This was the only way to know if the baby was really mine. The test was very expensive, and it cost more than half of all the money that I had.

When I went downstairs, Adam still hadn't moved.

"She's lovely," he said. "You're so lucky."

"Lucky?" He couldn't be serious.

"Yes. Because she'll love you without question – probably until she's about 13. That's when most kids realize that their parents are stupid."

"You know a lot for a 16-year-old."

"I may be shorter, younger and thinner than you. But I'm greater than you in every other way."

I laughed. It felt strange, but good. Adam was right. He was funny, smart, good-looking and did well in everything without trying. Not like me – I had to work really hard for everything I wanted.

———

When Adam was 12, he told me and Dad that he was going to be a famous actor.

"It's very difficult," Dad began. "What if you can't be an actor? You should have a Plan B."

"I don't need a Plan B," replied Adam. "A Plan B means that somewhere in my head, I think that I'll fail. But I'm too good to fail."

Dad and I looked at each other, but we didn't say anything.

———

"I'd love to be a dad one day," Adam said, looking down at Emma. "But it's not going to happen."

"When you meet the right girl . . ."

"If I meet the right person, it won't be a woman—"

"I don't want to talk about this, Adam," I said, turning away.

"No," he replied, "you never do."

"Look, you're too young to know who or what you really are. This is just a phase, and it'll pass. I just don't want you to get hurt," I told him. "You need to choose your moments."

"Do you mean the moments to talk about things that are important to me? Or the moments when you think that I should not?"

Was Adam trying not to understand me?

"Did you love Melanie?" Adam asked, unexpectedly.

I shook my head.

"That's sad," he replied. "Someone as special as your daughter should be . . . made with love."

Yes, Adam was right. Unlike me, Adam trusted everybody and everything until he had a reason not to. This was a beautiful thing, but it also made me worry about him.

Chapter Eleven

I am who I am

ADAM

Poor Dante. I feel so sorry for him.

It must be a real shock to suddenly discover that you're a dad and a single parent all in the same day. And the shock on his face when I said there was no chance of me becoming a dad!

I'm gay. But Dad thinks that if he doesn't notice it, then it'll go away. And Dante believes that it's just a phase.

I've known that I was gay since I was 13. I just wish that Dad and Dante would stop worrying about it and relax.

Chapter Twelve

Dad goes shopping

DANTE

Dad had bought so many things for Emma,
that the sitting room was full. There was a cot
which needed to be built and lots of nappies.
There was a high chair – a special chair with long
legs for Emma to sit at the table. There was a baby
carrier so you could carry a baby against your
chest while keeping your arms free to do other
things. There were also a lot of toys, baby creams,
baby spoons and forks, baby bottles, baby books
and baby clothes. Dad thought that the baby
was staying for a long time, but I knew that she'd
only be here until I got the DNA results.

"This must have cost so much money," I said,
shocked.

"I was only going to buy a cot, some nappies and a few clothes," Dad admitted. "But she's my granddaughter. Anyway, you'll have to buy everything after this."

That was another shock. I would have no money after a week.

Dad made Adam help him build the cot, so that I could spend time with Emma. Neither Adam nor I were happy with this plan, but Dad wouldn't listen.

"Do you really think she's mine?" The words came out before I could stop them.

Dad and Adam turned to look at me.

"Of course she's yours," said Adam. "She looks just like you."

"Adam's right," Dad said. "She looks just like you."

————

Forty minutes later, Dad came downstairs after making the cot. Emma was on the carpet playing with one of her new toys.

"Have you spoken to her?" he asked.

"To say what?" I asked.

Dad sighed. "Dante, she won't learn how to talk if you don't talk to her?"

"I know! I'm not completely stupid!"

"I never said that you were," Dad said, tiredly. "Not everything I say to you is meant in a negative way."

"But it is," I said, angrily. "When was the last time you said, 'Well done, Dante'?"

"Do you want praise for having a kid at 17? I'll praise you when you've done something to deserve it."

"Four A-stars so I can go to university wasn't enough?"

"I didn't say that. You did well," said Dad.

"I'll never do anything good enough for you, will I?"

"That's not true. But I wanted you to do something with your life, be someone."

"I'm sorry, I'm just a stupid 17-year-old with a kid. I'm sorry, Dad. Sorry, sorry, sorry."

"Don't shout at me . . ." Dad said.

Emma started crying very loudly and Adam came to the door. "I'm not surprised Emma's screaming. What the hell is wrong with you two?" he asked.

I picked up Emma and held her close. "Do you want me to take her?" Dad said.

"I don't need your help," I told him. "I can manage."

———

After this, Dad put the high chair together while Adam played with Emma and made her laugh. But as soon as Dad took the high chair into the kitchen, Adam turned to me angrily.

"What's wrong with you?" he said. "Dad's doing his best."

"Nothing," I said in a low voice. "But Dad didn't even say 'well done' when I told him my exam results."

"And you didn't even say 'thank you' for all the stuff that he bought Emma. The problem with you and Dad is that you're both stubborn. You're too alike."

"Are you crazy?" I said. "I'm not like him at all!"

When it was time to get Emma ready for bed, Dad could see that I was scared. "Do you need help?" he asked.

"Yes, please," I said, quietly.

"What did you say?" he asked, putting one hand behind his ear. "I didn't quite hear that."

Adam started to laugh and then Emma laughed too. Dad's mouth moved and then suddenly, we were all laughing together.

Dad showed me how to check that Emma's food wasn't too hot before feeding her, and how to give her a bath.

But she wouldn't lie down in her cot and go to sleep.

"Read or sing to her," Dad said. "That's what I used to do with you."

That was a surprise. Dad was a terrible singer. I didn't sing, but I read a book to Emma until she fell asleep.

———

Later, when everyone was sleeping, I switched on our computer and looked for my university. I stared at the computer for a long time, but I had to do this. I couldn't lose my future.

With a single click I accepted my place at the university.

Chapter Thirteen

Bar Belle

DANTE

The next morning, I woke up to the smell of poo and a noise that sounded like a cat crying – it was Emma. After I cleaned her and changed her nappy, I took her downstairs for breakfast.

"Hi, Emma," Adam smiled.

"Morning, dear," said Dad. I knew he wasn't talking to me. "I've made breakfast for you both."

"Great," I replied, putting Emma in her high chair. "I'm not hungry. Could you feed her please? I'm going back to bed."

"Not without your daughter," Dad said with a face like stone. "Where you go, she goes."

Emma knocked her breakfast on to the floor, then started to cry. While I cleaned up, Dad made more breakfast for her and Adam held her close until she was quiet.

I kept thinking – *What if I had to do this by myself? How had Melanie managed to do everything by herself, every single day?* I started to worry – Dad was going to a party after work and Adam was going shopping with his friends. This meant that I was going to be alone with Emma all day, and with no idea what to do with her. Dad was watching me carefully.

"OK, Dante," he said after a moment. "I'll stay at home with you, but only for today. This is the last time. And I'm still going to Louise's party."

"Really?" I turned and looked at Adam, and then said, "Thanks, Dad." And I meant it.

———

It was the end of school party at Bar Belle that evening, and my last chance to see some of my friends and celebrate before university. But Adam wouldn't babysit Emma for me, even when I said I'd pay him.

"Sorry," he said, "I'm meeting my friends at Bar Belle in forty minutes. I'm not the one with a kid and no life."

There was only one thing to do – I'd have to take Emma with me.

———

It was only 7.30 p.m., but Bar Belle was already

45

more than half full. Emma was asleep – for now – in her baby carrier. I probably wasn't right to bring her. But it was too late to think about that.

"Dante! We're over here."

Collette waved and smiled at me from a long table in the corner, where she was sitting with Josh, Logan and some other friends. She looked great. She was wearing a blood-red T-shirt, black jeans and long, gold earrings which were bright against her skin. Her hair was in a ponytail.

My friend Josh was sitting opposite her holding a bottle of beer, and from the happy look in his dark blue eyes, I knew it wasn't his first.

"So how is everyone?" I asked, acting like nothing was wrong. I sat down between Josh and Collette, but when I tried to kiss Collette, the baby carrier came between us.

"What's that?" Josh pointed at the baby carrier.

"What does it look like? A potato?"

"You brought a baby with you?" asked Logan.

Logan was slim and strong. He ran at least ten kilometres every day, either before or after school, and he liked to tell everybody, too.

"Whose baby is it?" Collette asked the one question that I did not want to hear.

"Er, she's a relative . . ." I said. "I have to look

46

after her, but I didn't want to miss this. Her name's Emma."

"Hi, Dante." Adam's voice came from behind me and my heart dropped. "Oh my God!" he said. "You brought Emma?" When I turned, he didn't look happy with me.

I wasn't planning to lie, but I wanted to tell my friends about Emma in my own way.

Adam gently touched Emma's cheek. "Can I wait with you until my friends arrive?" he asked.

"No, you can't!" said Josh. "You aren't invited."

I didn't want my brother with us either, but I didn't like how Josh had spoken to him.

"You heard him," Logan said. "Get lost!"

"Now wait a minute . . ." I began, but Adam put his hand on my shoulder.

"It doesn't matter, Dante. I'll see you later."

I looked up at Adam, but he and Josh were staring at each other – the same angry look on both their faces.

Then Adam walked away, and I turned to my friends.

"Josh, that's my brother you were talking to."

"He makes me nervous," Josh said.

"Why?" I asked.

"Because he does," Josh replied.

There was a strange silence around the table before Logan said, "We don't want a little kid with us."

Neither Josh nor Logan could quite look at me. Were they talking about all little kids or about my brother? Why didn't I ask Josh? Maybe I didn't want to know the answer. I'd been friends with Josh since I was ten and he was 11. Logan joined our school at 16, and I was surprised when Josh let him become part of our group.

Just then, Emma woke up, opened her eyes and started to cry. Suddenly, I saw the world the way she did. The music was too loud, the lights were too bright, and the bar smelled of beer.

"She's ugly, isn't she?" Logan said, watching her cry.

For a second, my heart stopped. I looked down at Emma as she cried. Adam was right. She was . . . beautiful.

Really beautiful.

"If you ever call my daughter ugly again, I'll punch your face!" I told Logan. Who was he to call Emma ugly?

He has a face like a horse!

"Your daughter?" Collette was the first to speak.

"Your daughter?" Josh repeated.

"Emma is my daughter and I'm taking her home. Have a great night everyone."

Collette followed me outside and she was

really angry.

"Why didn't you tell me that you had a daughter?"

"I didn't know until yesterday when Mel visited and left Emma with me. She didn't want Emma and neither do I," I said.

But as soon as I said the words, I was sorry.

"I have to go now," I said. "I'll phone you tomorrow."

I had to get my daughter home.

Chapter Fourteen

Toad face

ADAM

Josh is a horrible, little toad! I now know why he didn't want me to join Dante's group.

As soon as I walked past Josh's table on my way to the bar, he started saying stupid things. And each time he said something rude to me, Logan laughed louder and longer than necessary.

Logan thinks he's something special. But he's not. He's stupid!

Josh wasn't worth my time, and I wouldn't allow him to ruin my evening. I couldn't see Dante anywhere, maybe he'd done the right thing and taken Emma home.

"Are people like you allowed in here?" a voice whispered in my ear.

I knew it was Josh, even before I turned around.

"You think that you're smart, don't you?" he said.

"Don't forget good-looking, too," I told him before turning back to the bar.

To my surprise, Josh started to laugh. "You think a lot of yourself, don't you?"

"Yes. And I'm not the only one."

Josh laughed even more. And when I turned around, he was smiling at me. Was he feeling alright?

"I'll buy you a drink," he said.

But I wasn't stupid. I didn't know what Josh was planning, but I would be ready.

Chapter Fifteen

Being different

DANTE

It was only 9 a.m. but I was already tired because Emma hadn't slept all night – her new teeth were growing. I was in the kitchen trying to feed her when Adam walked in. As soon as he saw me, he tried to leave, but it was too late. I could see the angry-looking cut on one of his lips.

"What happened, Adam?"

"Nothing. I fell over."

"You fell on your face?"

"Why do you care? You didn't help me last night."

I immediately knew what he was talking about. "Yes, I did," I said. "I told Josh not to talk to you like that . . . Wait a moment, did Josh do that to you?"

"What would you do if Josh *had* done this?" Adam pointed to his mouth.

"I don't know, but I'd do something. No one does this to my brother."

Adam gave me a small smile. "Why do you spend time with Josh? He looks like a pink toad."

I started to laugh.

"And Logan's worse," he went on. "Why do you let Josh say and do anything he wants?"

"Like what?"

"Never mind!"

But I wanted to know. What was Adam trying to say? OK. Josh sometimes said stupid things, but he didn't really mean them. When we were at school, some older boys treated me badly, but Josh wouldn't let them hurt me. Although we didn't like the same books, films or music, we became good friends, and I learned to like what he did.

"You only see what you want to," Adam said.

"Did something happen at Bar Belle last night?"

"No." Adam turned away and I knew he was lying.

"Did your friends arrive?"

"Just Roxanne, Leanne and Anne."

53

Why did Adam only have girl friends? "Why can't you be more like other guys?"

"I lead, I don't follow," he told me. "I'm not afraid to be different. Not like some people."

"You'll get your arse kicked for being different."

"Sh!" he said. "Emma's listening."

"Adam! What happened to you?" Dad asked, coming into the kitchen.

"I fell."

"Don't your bloody eyes work?"

"Dad!" I said. "Don't use bad language in front of Emma!"

"Sorry, Emma," Dad said. "And Adam be more careful."

Just then, I heard the sound of the post arriving, and ran to get the letters before Dad and Adam could get to the door. The DNA tests were here.

Chapter Sixteen

What's wrong with me?

DANTE

I took the test up to my room and read the two pages of advice. I couldn't drink tea or coffee two hours before I did my test and Emma couldn't eat for two hours before her test. So now we both had to wait.

I could get the results by email or post. Email would be faster. But I shared a computer with Dad and Adam, so I decided to use the post. It would be slower, but safer.

As I was going downstairs the doorbell rang. It was Collette.

We needed to talk, so we decided to go to the park.

It was very hot, so we stopped at a shop to buy

drinks. As we waited to pay, the woman in front of us smiled when she saw Emma.

"Your sister's beautiful," she said.

"It's his daughter, not his sister," Collette replied.

Why did Collette say that?

The woman stopped smiling. "She's your *daughter*?"

She didn't say it quietly either. "How old are you?"

"Seventeen," I said slowly. I really didn't want to tell her.

The woman looked Collette up and down.

"Don't look at me," Collette said. "It's not my baby. I'm just a friend."

"Kids having kids," the woman said. "You probably don't even have a job!"

"You don't know anything about me," I said.

The woman gave me a dirty look. Then she turned away. I was so angry that I wanted to hit something. If Emma stayed with me, people would have a go at me. If she went away, it would be the same.

It didn't matter what I did, it would never be enough.

———

"What did people say about me last night?" I asked Collette when we arrived at the park.

"Some people were surprised and Josh – never mind," she said without looking at me.

"What did he say?"

"Josh said that living with Emma was probably the closest that Adam would get to the opposite sex."

"Josh said that to Adam?" I asked.

"You know what Josh is like when Logan's there pushing him. But don't worry, Adam told Josh where to go."

Why didn't Adam and Josh like each other? They laughed at the same things and they were both clever. What was their problem?

"Dante?" Collette's voice brought me back to the present. "What happens if Melanie doesn't come back?"

"I don't know," I replied.

"You had sex with Melanie and had a kid with her, but you've never wanted more than a kiss from me. What's wrong with me?"

"Nothing. I promise."

I took a moment to try and think of the right words. "What happened with Melanie happened once. We were both drunk and worried that somebody would interrupt . . . it wasn't the best—"

Collette nodded to show that she understood.

"I wanted our first time to be different, to be

something special. I thought that maybe at university where we both had our own rooms instead of living at home . . ."

"Oh, I see."

"But now there's Emma . . ."

"Yeah." Collette looked at Emma. "I really like you, Dante," she began. "But I've got plans and I'm going to university."

"I understand," I said, and I really did.

"It's not right that you have to forget your dreams," Collette said, angrily. "There must be something we can do."

"I don't see what," I said.

"I'll find something," she replied.

————

Back at home, I took Emma upstairs. I did the DNA tests and put them in their special envelope. Emma, who was sitting on the carpet "reading" one of her picture books, looked up at me and smiled. I looked down at her, trying to understand what I was feeling – but it was too confusing.

Later, when I went to the postbox, I stopped for a moment. I looked at the envelope in my hand and then at Emma who was in the buggy trying to eat her feet. What was stopping me? Before I could change my mind, I posted the envelope.

I was doing the right thing.

Wasn't I?

Chapter Seventeen

Aunt Jackie

DANTE

That evening, Aunt Jackie came to see me. When she stepped into the hall, Emma took one look at her and started to cry. Aunt Jackie was my mum's sister, so every time I saw her, I could see my mum's face. But where my mum had been like sunshine, Aunt Jackie was like a grey, wet day.

"You've been a busy boy," she said as soon as I opened the door.

"Hello, Aunt Jackie."

"I thought that you were more intelligent," she said. "But I suppose that you were thinking with what's in your trousers instead of your head."

Aunt Jackie carefully took Emma from me and

gently touched her hair and cheeks, but Emma wouldn't stop crying. "What's the matter with her?" she asked.

"She's teething."

"Poor little thing – are your teeth growing?" Aunt Jackie said. And then without pausing, "Dante, you look tired."

"I am," I admitted.

"Well, this is your life now. Just take it one day at a time."

"I'm trying, but it's so hard," my voice shook.

"And Emma has everyone's attention."

"Something like that," I admitted.

Then Aunt Jackie surprised me – she gently touched my face and said, "You were stupid, but you were also unlucky."

"What happens if I can't do this?"

"Every parent thinks that," she replied. "Just do your best. That's all anyone can do."

"Why didn't you have children?" I asked her.

My aunt paused before saying, "I really wanted to be a mum, but each time that I got pregnant I lost the baby. After the fourth time, I found out that I'd never have children."

"Is that why you and Uncle Peter aren't married any more?"

Aunt Jackie nodded. "We both really wanted to have a baby, but he could walk away. That's

60

life, Dante. Some people can walk away, and some people can't."

We looked at each other – I knew what she meant.

"Have you and your dad talked about how *you* feel?"

"No," I said. "Anyway, only girls talk about their feelings."

"Dante," Aunt Jackie said, "you and your dad are so alike."

Adam had said the same thing too and I didn't like it. Aunt Jackie gave Emma back to me and watched as I rested my head against hers for a moment.

"Trust yourself," she said.

When we went into the sitting room, Adam jumped up and gave Aunt Jackie a big hug. She looked at his mouth.

"Don't worry about this," Adam laughed. "I fell."

"Strange that you only hurt your mouth and nothing else."

She didn't believe him either.

"How are you?" she asked.

"I have a headache," he said, "but that's all. I'm fine."

Aunt Jackie watched as Emma pulled herself up using the armchair and then looked around at us.

"Walk to Daddy," Aunt Jackie said.

Emma immediately looked at me and my heart gave a big jump. She already knew who I was. I imagined Emma at the age of five or taking her to school . . . I imagined her staying.

"Come on, Emma. Walk to . . . me," I smiled.

She took three steps before falling into my arms.

But she had walked – to me.

"My clever little girl."

I held her high above my head. Then I remembered the letter I'd posted earlier and put her down on the carpet again. I had to be careful not to bond with her. When I looked up, Adam and Aunt Jackie were watching me.

Chapter Eighteen

She's yours

DANTE

Over the next few days, I used a timetable that Dad had made for me. It really helped me to know what I should be doing and when. But I still worried. Was I feeding Emma enough? Was she warm or cold? But even when I thought I'd made a mistake, Emma smiled at me or hugged me.

I loved watching her learn new things. I couldn't understand my feelings towards her. I had to be careful – I didn't want her inside my head.

Adam now had a secret. My brother hardly ever went out at night, but now he was going out every single night. He'd spend an hour in the shower and getting dressed, leave the house between 7.30 and 7.45 p.m. and return home at about 10 p.m. Dad didn't see this because he was working late, but I did.

"Where are you going again?" I asked.

"Why do you want to know?"

"Because something might happen to you," I replied.

"And how will that stop something from happening to me?" he asked.

"Aren't you going to tell me?"

"Dante," Adam said, as he was leaving. "Emma's your child, not me. See you later."

What was Adam's big secret?

But he was right – Emma was my child, and he wasn't.

———

Although I had Emma to look after, I tried to hold on to some of my old life. I phoned Collette – more than once – but I only got her voicemail. Josh was busy every night, and I could only go out if Dad was able to babysit.

———

Saturday morning brought rain, the postman and the DNA results.

"Dante, what's this?" Dad was looking down at the piece of paper in his hands.

"You opened my letter?"

"It said Mr Bridgeman, on the envelope, so I thought it was for me." Dad replied. "But then I read enough to realize that it wasn't. So, what is it?"

"They're the results of the DNA test that I did."

"Why? Anybody can see that Emma's your daughter."

"I needed to know for sure."

Dad was furious with me. "Are you going to keep having one test after another until you get the answer that you want?"

"No, Dad," I said. "And two days ago, I said 'no' to my university place."

That surprised him. "You did?"

"Yes. Call the university if you don't believe me. Everyone says that Emma looks like me. She laughs like Adam and she's stubborn like you, so she's definitely a Bridgeman. I don't need a piece of paper to tell me that."

I asked Dad to read the letter because I was afraid – but of what? That Emma was my daughter or that she wasn't?

Dad's lips started moving. Why couldn't I hear what he was saying?

"What did you say?" I asked.

"Emma's your daughter," smiled Dad.

I smiled at Emma and kissed her cheek.

Emma . . .

My daughter . . .
My daughter, Emma.

Chapter Nineteen

A family walk

DANTE

A couple of Saturdays after I got the DNA results, Dad, Adam, Emma and I went for a walk.

"I'll push Emma," said Dad, taking the buggy as soon as we left the house.

It felt strange for us all to be walking along together.

We hadn't gone to the park or the cinema in years.

"Why haven't we done this for a long time?" I asked Dad.

"When you started going out with your friends, you didn't want me with you. And then Adam copied you," said Dad.

That surprised me. Did I really make him feel unwanted? "I'm sorry, Dad," I said, quietly.

"And, I never said thank you properly for all the stuff you bought for Emma and for helping me with her."

Now Dad looked surprised – but pleased. "That's OK!" he smiled.

I smiled back.

"Hi!" said Adam to a woman who was passing.

"Morning."

"Lovely day."

"Adam! Do you have to speak to everybody that we meet?" I asked.

"I can say hello to people if I want to," he replied.

"Hi."

"How are you?"

He didn't stop until I put my hand over his mouth.

"I'll let you go when you promise to stop being so happy," I told him.

Finally, he nodded. But as soon as I let him go, he ran off and then turned round to face us.

"Hello, world!" he shouted, making me laugh.

"Dante, it's good to hear you laugh again," said Dad.

It felt good, too.

Chapter Twenty

Happy and sad

ADAM

How is it possible to be so happy and so sad at the same time?

I've met someone. And when we're alone, he's great. He's smart and makes me laugh so much.

But when others are around, it's a different story.

I wish that he wasn't so ashamed of me.

And if he could stop feeling so ashamed of himself, then maybe we might have a chance.

Chapter Twenty-one

Veronica's visit

DANTE

It took me a moment to recognize the woman at the door. It was Collette's sister, Veronica. But what did she want?

We went into the sitting room where Emma was playing on the floor. I could smell Emma's nappy from where I stood. Should I change her now or wait until Veronica left? I didn't want to appear rude, so I decided to wait. Veronica sat opposite me on the sofa.

"I don't know if Collette told you, but I'm a social worker."

I had a bad feeling about this . . .

"She also told me that a girlfriend . . . Melanie . . . left a child with you . . ." Veronica looked at

Emma quickly. "And now you're having to manage the baby alone?"

"I'm not alone. My dad and my brother are helping me. Excuse me, but why are you here?"

"Collette said you were unhappy about this."

"I was at the beginning, but not now."

"But you're going to university," she said.

"No. I'm not going to university any more."

"Oh," she said, surprised. "So what are you going to do?"

"I'm going to find a job."

"And who will look after your daughter when you get a job? What will you do when she's ill?"

Veronica asked lots of questions, one after another.

I answered them all and tried not to show that I was angry.

"Are you managing, Dante?" she asked.

"What do you mean?"

"I can smell that Emma's nappy needs changing, but you're not doing anything about it."

Calm down, Dante. Don't get angry.

"I know it needs changing, but I was waiting until you left. I didn't think you'd be staying so long."

"Don't let me stop you," she replied.

I quickly changed Emma's nappy without

saying another word. As I was finishing, Veronica said, "Dante, I want to help you."

It didn't feel like it.

"Have you decided to keep Emma with you?"

"She's my daughter," I said. "I've only had her a few weeks and I'm still learning, but I know I could be a good dad if I'm given the chance."

"You're only 17. Nobody expects you to be as patient as an older person, or to have the same ability."

I didn't agree with her. "There are plenty of older parents who hurt their kids or who don't care about them," I said. "I'll be 18 in two weeks and all my family want to make this work."

"Good," said Veronica. "Because if I don't think that this is a good place for Emma, there are a few things that I can do."

I picked Emma up and held her close. "Would you be talking to me like this if I was Emma's mum instead of her dad?" I said, angrily.

"What do you mean?" asked Veronica.

"You think that because I'm Emma's dad and not her mum, that I must be failing. Well, let's talk about Melanie. She didn't tell me that she was pregnant or when Emma was born. She came here, left the baby and then went away without leaving an address! And you're ready to get at me – just because of my age and because

I'm a man."

"Dante, I'm on your side," Veronica replied. "I can see that you've already bonded with Emma, but there are other things for you to think about. For example, does Emma have a doctor?"

"I'll register her tomorrow," I said. "But Emma's staying with me."

Veronica gave me her business card and told me to call her if I needed help. I walked her to the door without speaking.

"I'll be back in a few weeks to talk to you and your dad," she said, "just to see how you're all doing." Then she left.

Was that a threat or a promise?

Chapter Twenty-two

You don't want her

DANTE

I called Dad immediately. "They'd only take Emma away if she was in danger," he said. "She isn't, so don't worry. But I'll come home now if you need me."

"That's OK. But thanks, Dad."

It felt great to have Dad's help. For the first time, I thought about his life after Mum died of cancer. Two boys to bring up and bills to pay. I needed to find a job quickly. But first, I had to make another phone call.

"Collette?"

"Hello?"

"Your sister's just left."

"Good. I told her you needed help."

"Why did you tell her about me and Emma?"

"I was trying to help. This way, the baby can go to a different family and you can go to university. I've only seen you three times since she arrived, and we can't do anything that we'd planned."

I tried to stay calm. "Her name's Emma and she's my daughter."

"But you don't want her . . ."

Collette didn't seem to understand why I was so angry.

"I'm only going to say this once, Collette. Emma's my daughter. I've bonded with her and she belongs with me. If you don't like that, that's your problem. And in future, you and Veronica can keep out of my life! Enjoy university."

I ended the call and then looked at Emma.

"You're staying with Daddy," I told her. "I promise."

Chapter Twenty-three

Enough

ADAM

I can't do this any more.

Why did he even ask me out? It was his idea for us to get together – not mine. I want to live my life out loud, not whisper through life like he does, hoping that no one will notice him.

I can't live my life like that.

I won't.

I really like him, but I think . . . I think it's time to end things.

This will never work until he learns to be happy with who and what he really is. But I'm beginning to think that's never going to happen.

And I'm getting tired of waiting.

Chapter Twenty-four

At the doctor's

DANTE

It was more difficult to register Emma with my doctor than I'd thought. The first time I went there, I couldn't register her because I didn't have her medical card, her birth certificate or the red book with her medical notes.

I didn't have anything to show who I was either. The receptionist thought that I was Emma's brother, and not her father, and told me to come back with my mum.

When I returned home, I found the red book in the big envelope of papers that Mel had left. There were notes about Emma's birth and lots of useful information about babies. If I wanted to keep Emma – and I did – then there were a lot of things that I needed to do.

Chapter Twenty-five

Leave me alone

ADAM

Oh God! I want him to stop phoning me and texting me and sending me emails and messages. It's making me crazy. I'm beginning to be afraid to turn on my phone.

It's finished.

Why doesn't he understand? Does he think this is easy for me? This isn't what I wanted.

I was stupid.

This is what he wanted – a boring life without problems.

Why can't he just let me live in peace?

Chapter Twenty-six

Happy birthday

DANTE

Six weeks later, it was Emma's first birthday. We had a little party for her. It was great. She had a birthday cake and lots of presents from Dad, Aunt Jackie and Adam. Dad finally got his camera out and took lots of photos. It was just like old times and I couldn't stop smiling.

———

A week later it was my eighteenth birthday, but I didn't need a cake or want presents. Dad said that he'd babysit and gave me some money so that I could go out and celebrate with Adam.

Bar Belle was very busy for a Wednesday. I wanted to go somewhere else, but Adam wanted to stay.

"Hey, Dante!"

I turned around to see Josh, Paul and Logan standing behind us. I was surprised to see Logan – I thought that he was at university. Paul had a job, but I didn't know what Josh was doing.

"Hey, guys," I said.

"Hi, Josh," said Adam.

"Dante." Josh didn't look at my brother. Instead, he spoke to me. "I haven't seen you in a while."

"My brother just said 'hello' to you," I replied.

"I know," Josh said. "I heard him."

"Then you should bloody answer him," I said.

"It's OK," Adam said.

But it wasn't OK. I didn't like the way that Josh spoke about Adam.

"*Hello*, Adam," Josh said. "How's it going? Are you happy now, Dante?"

"Relax, guys," Paul said.

I turned to Logan, "I thought that you were going to university."

"Not for another week," he replied.

When I turned back, Josh was staring at my brother, but Adam didn't look at him. "Are you OK, Josh?" I asked.

"I'm fine. What've you been doing?"

"I've been looking after my daughter."

"And what else?" he asked.

Now I understood why Melanie had smiled when I asked her the same question. Looking after a small child was a full-time job.

"We're celebrating Dante's birthday. Do you want to join us?" asked Adam.

I gave Adam a hard look, but Paul was smiling like it was the best idea ever. Logan was watching Josh. And Josh looked as unhappy as me at the idea.

The conversation was slow at first, but soon we were chatting and laughing. The only problem was that my friends were drinking beer like it was water and throwing fries at each other. If this went on, the manager would ask us to leave.

"Josh, can I try one of your fries?" Adam asked, his hand already over Josh's plate.

Josh twisted Adam's arm hard. "I don't want your hand in my food, you gay . . ."

"Josh!" Adam said in shock.

We were all shocked into silence for a moment. I was having trouble breathing and I knew that Adam was close to crying.

"Let go of my brother. *Now*!"

"Sorry, Dante, but I really don't want your brother touching my food. I don't know what I might catch."

I moved towards Josh, my eyes full of threat,

but Adam jumped up and stopped me.

"He's not worth it, Dante," Adam told me. "He's a coward. A scared little kid afraid of everything and everyone."

"Don't you ever talk to my brother like that again," I hissed at Josh.

"Josh," Logan began. "What did Adam mean? Is there something that you want to tell us?"

Josh was on his feet now. The manager came to our table and told us to stop arguing or leave. I looked at the others. Paul looked surprised at what was happening. Josh was ready to fight, but Logan was smiling. A small secret smile that was for Josh alone.

As soon as Paul, Josh and Logan left the restaurant, Adam sat down. When I put my hand on his shoulder, he was shaking and trying not to show it. I was glad the others had gone.

Until I realized that they had left me to pay the bill.

Bastards!

Chapter Twenty-seven

The attack

DANTE

I was still angry when Adam and I walked home. Because of that bill, I had no money left. And I was furious about what Josh had said to my brother. We were nearly home when . . .

Time stopped.

Suddenly I was on the ground unable to move because somebody was lying on my legs and holding my arms back.

I looked up to see Josh pushing Adam against the wall of a house.

"Leave him alone, Josh," I shouted.

But Josh just laughed, and Logan and Paul pulled my arms back even harder.

Every time Adam tried to stand up straight,

Josh pushed him again. But Adam never took his eyes off Josh – not once.

"You're horrible and dirty. You make me sick," Josh hissed.

Each word hit me like a punch, but Adam didn't say a word.

Instead, he did something that made the world stop turning.

Adam kissed Josh full on his mouth.

Josh didn't speak or move. But only for a moment. Then he went crazy.

Using his fists, he kept punching Adam's face again and again. Adam tried to protect himself, but there was nothing he could do. He fell to the ground, rolling into a ball, with his arms still up by his head. Then Josh started to kick my brother's head. Again. And again. And again.

I tried to get free, but Logan was on my back and Paul was on my knees.

"You always thought you were better than us – going to go to university to be a journalist. Look at you now!"

Logan hissed in my ear. "You're a nobody with a kid, no job and a gay brother."

I couldn't move. All I could see was Josh and my brother. And Adam wasn't moving.

"GET OFF HIM. JOSH, YOU BASTARD. STOP. YOU'RE KILLING HIM!"

84

Paul jumped up and tried to pull Josh away, but he wasn't strong enough. And when he asked Logan for help, Logan didn't move.

As soon as I was free, I punched Logan on the side of the head and then kicked him a couple of times. Then I put my arm around Josh's neck and pulled him back so fast and hard that his feet didn't touch the ground. After that, I ran back to Adam.

"Adam . . .?" I whispered. I put my ear down towards his mouth and nose. Was he breathing?

"Josh," Paul pulled him away. "We have to leave. Now!"

"What's happening?" A man came out of the nearest house. "Zoe, call the police," he called over his shoulder.

"Leave now or I'll kill you." I looked into Josh's eyes. "I promise." I spoke quietly, but I meant every single word. Then I dropped down to my knees.

Adam's face was all blood and bone. I didn't know what to do.

"Adam," I gently touched his head, "please don't die. Please don't die."

Chapter Twenty-eight

The hospital

DANTE

Time moves very slowly when you're waiting for news in a hospital.

Two policewomen came and asked me lots of questions.

"Did you see the people who did this?"

I don't know why, but for a moment I paused. And then quickly, before I could change my mind, I said "Josh Davies, Logan Pane and Paul Anders. They were drinking beer all night. Logan and Paul held me down, but it was Josh who hurt my brother. He kept punching and kicking Adam in the head."

I felt sick talking about it.

"So you were all at Bar Belle together?" asked one of the policewomen.

"It wasn't the plan. Adam and I were already there. We shared a table and then they started to argue with us. They left before we did."

They questioned me for another twenty minutes and wrote down *every* word that I said, before they left.

Now I was sitting in hospital. Was my brother going to live or die?

———

All the way to the hospital, the ambulance workers fought to save my brother's life. I was scared that if I looked away, even for a moment, I would lose Adam for ever. As soon as we arrived at the hospital, they took Adam away for an operation and I called Dad.

"Hi, Dante," Dad said, brightly. "Did you have a good time? Are you on your way home? It's getting late."

"Dad. I'm at the hospital. It's Adam. He was attacked in the street. He's badly hurt."

"I'm on my way," Dad said, and put down the phone.

———

Dad arrived about forty minutes later, with Emma asleep in his arms.

"This is what I've always been afraid of," he said, quietly, after I told him everything that had happened.

87

We sat in silence for a long time.

"What happened?" Aunt Jackie asked as soon as she arrived.

"Adam was attacked for being gay," Dad said. "I thought that didn't happen today. This is the 21st century – or at least it's supposed to be."

I couldn't look at Dad or my aunt.

"Why did you let this happen?" asked Dad.

"I tried to stop it, Dad."

"You should have tried harder."

"Stop it, Tyler," Aunt Jackie said to Dad. "That's not helping."

"Keep out of this, Jackie," Dad told her. "It's my son who's fighting for his life."

"And the son sitting next to you needs a kind word from his dad," replied Aunt Jackie.

I got up and went to the men's toilet before Dad or Aunt Jackie could stop me. I washed my hands and my face, then looked in the mirror. My eyes were bright with tears.

I felt terrible about all of this. I had never stopped Josh when he said horrible things about people from other countries and religions – he hated everybody. Who knows what he said about me and other black people behind my back?

Adam had called Josh a coward, but I was one, too. I turned away from the mirror, unable to look at myself a moment longer. When I got back, Aunt Jackie and Dad were arguing about me. And what I heard explained so much – too much.

————

"So you only married Mum because she was pregnant . . . with me?" I said to Dad. "That's why nothing I ever did was good enough. You think that I ruined your life."

Dad gave Emma to Aunt Jackie and walked over to me.

"Dante, it's true that your mum and I probably only got married because of you at that time. I was only twenty and at university. But she was pregnant, and I really cared about you and your mum. I still do."

"But Adam was born with love – I wasn't."

"Listen to me, Dante. If I've ever made you feel like I didn't love you, then I'm sorry. Because that's not true. It's never, never been true. And if I pushed you too hard, it's because I didn't want you to make my mistakes."

"And I was your biggest mistake."

I tried to turn away, but Dad wouldn't let me.

"Sometimes, the things you think that you don't want, are really the things that you need most in the world," he said. "You have Emma, so you know what I mean. You, Adam and your mum are the only things in my life that I've ever cared about. When your mum got pregnant, I was going to finish university and maybe work as a film editor. That didn't happen. But if I could go back and live my life again, I wouldn't change a thing." He looked at me. "Do you believe me, Dante? It's really important that you believe me?"

"Mr Bridgeman?" The doctor appeared, saving me from having to reply.

"Is Adam OK?" asked Dad.

"He has many serious injuries, but he's alive. His jaw and his nose were broken, but we've saved his right eye. It'll take a long time for his face to get better and he'll have some permanent scars. Come with me."

———

"Oh my God!" said Dad.

Next to me, Aunt Jackie started to cry.

I could only stare. I didn't recognize Adam's face. There was a bandage around his head and jaw, and his face was swollen and out of shape.

My beautiful brother, Adam.

Just wait until I found Josh . . .

Chapter Twenty-nine

Proud of you

DANTE

Two days later, when we went to visit Adam, his bed was empty . . .

"Where's my son?" Dad shouted, running towards two nurses.

"I'm sorry, Mr Bridgeman," said one of the nurses. "I wanted to speak to you before you reached his bed. Please come with me."

My whole body went cold.

"Where's my son?" Dad repeated, but this time his voice was very quiet.

We went into a small waiting room and sat down. "Adam had a haematoma in his head, but we don't think this is because of the attack. Luckily, Adam was already here in hospital, so we operated immediately. Has Adam been having headaches?"

"Yes," Dad said. "We've been waiting for a scan for weeks. He was playing football, and the ball hit him in the head. But I don't understand . . ."

"It wasn't a football, Dad. It was a cricket ball!"

"Cricket balls are hard," the nurse said. "I see. That explains everything."

"Will he be. . . OK?" I had to ask.

The nurse smiled, "It's not a dangerous operation. I'll let you know as soon as I have more news."

After she left, Dad and I watched Emma play for a while.

"Do you think that Veronica will hear about this?" I asked.

I'd been thinking about that for days.

"Stop worrying about Veronica," Dad said. "Emma isn't going anywhere."

I picked Emma up and held her close. When I turned, Dad was watching me.

"Dante, I want you to know how proud of you I am. I'm proud of how well you did in your exams. And I'm proud of the way you've become a real father to Emma."

"Thanks, Dad," I said, quietly.

"And I want you to know – I love you, son. Very much."

Dad was looking straight ahead and not at me, but I believed him. He'd never told me that before, but I'd never said those words to him either. I guess that Dad and I were alike.

"I . . . I love you too Dad."

Chapter Thirty

Paul

DANTE

"Where is he, Paul?" I held him to the ground, so that he couldn't move.

"I don't know," he replied, trying to get away.

Over a month had passed since Adam's second operation. He'd spent eight days in hospital, but the people who had hurt him were still free. At home, Adam never left his bedroom except to go to the bathroom, and he was always in pain. He stopped speaking and wrote us messages instead. The right side of his face looked terrible. He had lots of scars, and his right eye drooped. The doctors said that it might get better with time, but Adam didn't care any more. I was tired of waiting for the police to do their jobs, so I decided to take action myself. It was easy to discover where Paul worked.

———

"If you don't tell me where Josh is," I threatened Paul, "I'll . . ."

"He's at Logan's," Paul said, quickly.

"Liar! Logan's at university now."

"No, he's not. He didn't get the right results. Logan's the liar, not me."

Despite everything, I believed him. When I got to my feet, Paul tried to sit up.

"I'm sorry about your brother . . ." he began.

"Don't you talk about my brother!" I said. "Are you going to tell Josh that I'm looking for him?"

"He already knows. That's why he doesn't stay in the same place for very long."

"Did the police come and see you?"

"Yes, me and Logan. We'll have to go to court."

"And Josh?"

"The police haven't caught him yet."

This wasn't good enough. I needed to find him.

"Don't tell Josh that I'm looking for him," I said as I walked away.

"It wasn't Josh," Paul called after me. "Yes, he hurt Adam, but it was Logan who . . ."

"Who did what?"

Paul tried to make himself small when he saw the look on my face.

"Logan kept saying that Josh was . . . was the same as Adam. That made Josh furious, and then he said he'd show us that he hated gay people, that he wasn't . . ."

"I get the picture."

"Josh did it because Logan kept pushing him . . ."

I remembered what Collette had told me in the park. *You know what Josh is like when Logan is pushing him.*

Was I wrong? Should I be looking for Logan instead of Josh?

I decided to find Josh first, then that other bastard – Logan.

Chapter Thirty-one

Finding Josh

DANTE

I found Josh on the second night. It was easier than I thought. He was walking down Logan's road with a rucksack on his back and wearing jeans, a dirty T-shirt and the brown jacket he got for his sixteenth birthday. He had his head down, but as soon as he saw me, he began to run.

He was fast.

But I was faster.

I threw him against the nearest wall as hard as I could.

"I'm sorry . . ." Josh tried to stop me putting my hands around his neck. "I didn't mean to . . . But when he kissed me . . ."

I pressed my hands against Josh's neck – hard. His face began to turn dark red, but I didn't stop

– I was doing this for Adam. Just as Josh's eyes were beginning to close, he suddenly stopped pulling away from me . . .

And kissed me.

I let go of him immediately and wiped my mouth with the back of my hand. Josh fell to the ground, trying to breathe.

"I'm going to kill you!" I shouted and started punching his face hard. He tried to push me away, but I didn't stop.

"See," he said, speaking through a mouth full of blood. "You hate us gay people just as much as I do."

Us gay people?

Then he started to cry.

"You're . . . you're *gay*?"

Still crying, Josh nodded.

"I don't hate . . . I'm not like you," I began. "This is about what you did to Adam."

But was I being honest with myself? I thought that I hated Josh because of what he had done to my brother. But that was nothing to how I felt when Josh kissed me.

So what did that make me? I tried to understand how I felt.

Josh slowly got to his feet. He was still crying.

"Is . . . is Adam going to be OK?"

I couldn't believe it! He'd nearly killed my

brother and now he was asking if Adam was well.

"Could you tell him that I'm sorry?" asked Josh.

I just turned and walked away without saying another word.

Chapter Thirty-two

The doctor visits

DANTE

I wasn't the only one that was worried about Adam. Even after the bandages came off his jaw he hardly spoke or left his room. He wouldn't see any of his friends when they visited, and after two or three times, they stopped coming.

The left side of Adam's face now looked normal, but he had many scars on the right side. And he could only see a little with his right eye. When Emma tried to go into his room, he screamed at her to leave.

"Don't shout at her," I told Adam. "She misses you."

When Emma stopped crying, I tried to explain to her. "Your uncle isn't feeling well at the moment. Something happened to his face and his heart is hurting."

Poor Adam.

Two days later, we got some good news. The police told us that Josh had visited them. I told Adam, but he didn't seem to care.

My brother was broken, and I didn't know how to fix him.

———

Winter came and went with no change in our lives. I still couldn't find a job, Dad was working extra hours and Adam wouldn't even come downstairs to spend Christmas with us. Sometimes, at night, I could hear him walking up and down in his room. And once or twice, I thought that I heard him crying.

After the Christmas holidays, Adam wouldn't go back to school. Dad was so worried that he called the doctor.

After visiting Adam, the doctor decided that Adam wasn't ready for school. She gave him some pills to help him sleep – just enough for two weeks. Dad was unhappy about this.

"I'll keep the pills and give one to Adam to take each night," he said. "Then he can't take two in the night by mistake. You know what he's like with pills."

Chapter Thirty-three

This is my life

ADAM

Somebody's knocking at my door again. Is it Dad or Dante?

It doesn't matter. Why don't they understand that I don't want to see either of them?

I'm so tired. Maybe the sleeping pills that the doctor gave me will help.

Here I am in my room, with my future lying in front of me like a desert without end.

This is my life.

A life that I'm too scarred and scared to let anyone see.

Chapter Thirty-four

Veronica returns

DANTE

After two weeks, Adam said that the sleeping pills had worked and that he didn't need anything else. He wouldn't see the doctor and he wouldn't leave his room either.

So we carried on as normal.

Dad took another day off work when Veronica, the social worker, visited us again to 'discuss' Emma's future.

"Remember you're doing this for Emma," Dad said, before Veronica arrived. "Don't get angry."

Veronica stayed at our house for about an hour. She asked lots of questions, but she also gave me lots of good advice. I showed her Emma's medical book – I had registered Emma at the doctor's and all her vaccinations were done. Veronica told me what to do to get Emma's child support money so that it came to me instead of going to Melanie. Child support was money that was given to parents to buy clothes and food for children. This was important, because I didn't have a job. She also told me how to change Emma's birth certificate, so that my name was on the document. It was better to do this before Emma was two years old, because after that it would be more difficult.

Just before she left, we went upstairs to see Emma, who was still sleeping.

"Is she talking yet?" asked Veronica.

"Yes, she says quite a few words and more every day," I said.

"She's very important to you, isn't she?" Veronica asked.

"Yes. She's my world."

Chapter Thirty-five

Spring

DANTE

Spring had finally arrived, and it was the day before Adam's birthday. When I went to his room, he was sitting with his back to the door as usual.

"What do you want for your birthday?" I asked.

"Can I have a mirror?" he said.

"What? Now?"

I was sure that I hadn't heard Adam correctly, but he repeated the question. I wasn't sure what to do, but Dad was at work and I couldn't ask him. Maybe Adam was finally getting better, so I went to get the bathroom mirror.

Time stood still as Adam looked at himself.

The right side of his face was looking better. The skin looked softer and smoother and his scars were disappearing, but his right eye was still drooping.

"I'm not going to be an actor, am I?" he finally said.

"What do you mean?" I put the mirror down. "You can still be an actor. You can be anything that you want to. Anyway, there are lots of other things that you can do, too."

"I never made a Plan B, remember?"

"You can make one now."

After a long pause I asked the question that had been in my head for months.

"Why did you kiss Josh?"

"Because . . . because he kissed me first."

I stared at Adam in shock.

"It was the night that you took Emma to Bar Belle. After you left, Josh tried to kiss me. I wouldn't let him, so he punched me instead."

"Your cut lip," I said.

"The day after, Josh rang me to say sorry and invited me out for a drink. After that we started going out together."

"You and . . . *Josh*?"

"We just did normal things – like having a meal or going to the cinema. I was so happy, Dante. I thought that I'd found someone and that we were together."

I didn't know what to say. I remembered the time when Adam was going out every night and seemed really happy.

"But Josh hated to be seen with me and kept saying horrible things about gay people when other people were around. I really liked him, Dante, but I couldn't be with someone who was living a lie like that . . . so I left him."

"You did *what*?"

Adam gave a small smile. "But he kept phoning me, so I blocked his calls. I think that's what made him so angry."

Now I was beginning to understand the strange looks and the bad feeling between them. Adam was gay and didn't care who knew it, but Josh was the opposite. When he said negative things about gay people, the person he really hated most was himself.

"I can't believe it!" I said. "Being gay isn't an illness! You're either born gay or you're not born gay and are heterosexual – end of conversation."

"And if you're bisexual?"

"Then you like both boys and girls – no problem."

"So being gay isn't just a phase?"

"Of course not. What are you . . . ?" And then I remembered our conversation from so long ago.

Adam smiled – he thought he was so clever.

"Do you still think about Josh?" I asked.

"All the time."

"Do you think that it would be better to try and forget him?" I chose my words carefully.

"How can I forget, Dante? Every time I touch my face or take a breath, I remember."

When we were young, if Adam hurt himself, I could make him feel better. But that was when we were young.

"Josh sent me a letter," Adam said. "He's not doing very well."

"Who cares?" I said, angrily. "Where's his letter?"

"I threw it away."

"Good. What else did he say?"

"He said that he was sorry."

Adam went and sat back down in his chair. His shoulders drooped and I hated seeing him like that.

Just as I was asking him how much longer he was going to stay in his room, Emma came to the bedroom door.

"Daddy?"

I was very surprised that she could now get upstairs by herself. She hadn't seen Adam for weeks, and he quickly turned so that we couldn't see his face.

"Heyo, Unckey," – her words for "Hello, Uncle."

She walked to Adam, waving her arms at him and smiling. "Heyo, Unckey," she repeated. "Heyo."

Slowly, Adam picked her up. Emma reached out one small hand and gently touched the scars on his face.

"Hurts?" she asked.

"Yes," Adam whispered.

"Lots?"

"Lots."

"Kiss?"

Adam sighed, then smiled – the first real smile that I'd seen from him in a long, long time.

"Yes, please," he said.

She bent forward and kissed his scarred cheek. Then she hugged him hard.

And from where I was standing, I could see that Adam was crying.

Chapter Thirty-six

Just like Mum used to do

ADAM

Emma pressed her good cheek against my bad one and hugged me like she'd never let me go.

I started to cry, and I couldn't stop, and still Emma held me. She just kissed my cheek and hugged me some more.

What hurt most was that it was like when Mum used to hold me.

Chapter Thirty-seven

Wake up!

DANTE

When I woke up the next morning, I felt great. Things were finally getting better for us. Adam had let Emma see his face and I was hoping to start work at the local petrol station. At least now I could make some money.

I knocked on Adam's door to wake him for breakfast. There was no answer, so I went in.

"Wake up, birthday boy! Breakfast's ready."

There was still no answer, but as I walked to his bed, I stepped on a little piece of a pill – a sleeping pill . . . But hadn't Adam finished those months ago?

"Adam?" I shook him as hard as I could. "*Wake up!*" But he didn't move, and his eyes were closed.

"ADAM? ADAM, WAKE UP!" I shouted. "DAD . . ."

Dad came running into the room. His face turned grey when I showed him the pill. Quickly, he bent his head to check if my brother was breathing.

"Call an ambulance now!"

I didn't need to be told twice. I phoned them while Dad pulled Adam off the bed and started walking him up and down.

"Adam, walk! Do you hear me?" Dad ordered. "*Walk!*"

"Daddy?" cried Emma from downstairs.

I wanted to stay with Dad and Adam, but Dad said, "Dante, go. Emma needs you."

As soon as I got downstairs, Emma stopped crying and held out her arms. I took her out of her high chair.

"Park," said Emma.

"Not today. We'll go another day," I tried to explain as she started to cry again.

'Park," she said, crying even more loudly.

"No."

"Park . . . park . . . park . . ." she repeated in between cries until I couldn't take any more.

"EMMA! SHUT UP!"

And she did, for one shocked moment. Then she really started to scream.

I could feel myself getting angrier and angrier and my hands becoming fists.

I didn't trust myself, so I ran from the kitchen and into the sitting room. I couldn't believe what I'd nearly done.

When I was calmer, I went back to Emma and picked her up.

"I'm sorry," I said. "I was worried about Uncle Adam."

"Poor Unckey," Emma sighed.

"Yes," I said, when I could trust myself to speak.

Chapter Thirty-eight

The letter

DANTE

While Dad and Adam were at the hospital, I called Aunt Jackie. I was scared of what I might do if Emma started crying again. She wasn't pleased.

"Dante? Do you know what time it is? I don't get up early on Saturdays."

"Aunt Jackie, I . . . I need your help . . ."

Why were the words so hard to say? Then I told her everything – about Adam and the sleeping pills, and about me shouting at Emma and what I'd almost done.

"I'll be there as soon as I can," she said.

After I spoke to Aunt Jackie, I went upstairs to Adam's room – it made me feel closer to him. As I was making his bed, I found a piece of paper – it was the letter from Josh.

Adam,

I know I'm probably the last person you want to hear from, but I hope you'll read this letter.

I'll be in court soon. The police have photos and doctors' reports of your injuries, so I'll probably go to prison because of what I did to you. Mum has washed her hands of me and my friends don't want to know me any more.

You were right – I'm a coward. But I need to say this to you. I'm really, really sorry about what I did to you. Even now when I think about it, I can't believe what I did.

Can I ask you a favour? Will you write to me in prison? I'll send you my address, but I'll understand if you don't want to. Isn't it strange? I thought I'd lose all my friends if they knew I was gay, but I've lost them anyway.

I heard you haven't returned to school yet. Is it because, like me, you feel dead inside – like there's no reason for living?

I told you things I've never told another person – ever. I told you I cared about you. That's still true, but I still hurt you. Now you think the world is full of two-faced people and liars like me, so what's the point? Every second of every day I'm sorry for what I did. I hope you'll write back to me – but if you won't

or don't or can't, I'll understand.
  Take care of yourself.
  Your friend,
  Joshua

I read the letter again, but it left me more confused. So Adam hadn't thrown the letter away. Was this why he'd taken those pills after all this time? Was Josh right about how Adam must be feeling? I put the letter back. Had the letter made him think about his old worries or had it shown that they hadn't got better?

————

"Where's Emma?" Aunt Jackie asked as soon as she arrived.

"In the sitting room – she's drawing."

"I'm so proud of you," she said. "You didn't hit Emma. You walked away when you got angry and gave yourself a chance to calm down."

"But I nearly . . ."

"If 'nearly' was important, most adults would be in prison! Well done for asking for help when you needed it."

Aunt Jackie smiled when she saw the look on my face. "Men think it's not strong to ask for help. Look at Adam," Aunt Jackie sighed. "Alone in his room for months. Too much of a man to tell anyone how he really felt."

"I'm not going to let that happen again. I love Adam too much," I said.

"Have you told him?"

"No, I haven't . . . but he knows."

"Just like you know your dad loves you," Aunt Jackie looked at me to see if I understood what she was saying. "I'm sure you like hearing the words though."

"Daddy?" Emma called.

"Where's my baby?" Aunt Jackie said, pushing me to one side as she ran into the sitting room to be with my daughter.

I thought about what Aunt Jackie had said, about men not asking for help. I wasn't the only guy to become a single dad at 18, and there wasn't a lot of information written for us. I had an idea – maybe I could do something about it. But for now, I had other things to worry about.

Chapter Thirty-nine

Real men cry

DANTE

Dad looked at least five years older when he returned home with Adam that evening. Adam didn't look any different.

"Hi, Adam."

"Hi, Dante," he whispered.

"Are you OK?" Aunt Jackie asked.

"I'm fine," he said, and then went straight to his room.

Dad told us what the doctor had said at the hospital.

It was lucky that Adam had taken the pills early that morning and not the night before. They hadn't stayed in his blood for long. But if . . . Dad shook his head.

I went upstairs to see Adam. There was

something that I needed to say to him.

"I don't remember inviting you in," he said, when I entered his room. "I want to be alone."

No. I would not let this happen – not any more.

"I read Josh's letter," I told him.

"You had no right," Adam said.

"Neither did you."

We both knew that I wasn't talking about reading Josh's letter.

Adam turned. "Look at my face. I can't live like this."

"You're more than your face," I said. "Is that why you did it?"

"No. I did it because Josh is right. What's the point?"

"The point is you have family and friends who love you. You have a world out there waiting for you. You have a life that can be anything you want it to be."

"But the world's full of people like Josh – people who hate everyone. They even hate themselves," Adam sighed.

"That's why you can't let them win. Don't let them ruin your life."

"I'm tired, Dante. And I'm scared."

"Everyone's scared, Adam."

"You're not. You're like Dad. You carry on with

life and it doesn't matter what it throws at you."

"I'm scared of Melanie coming back and taking Emma . . . And I'm scared of losing you."

Adam looked down at his hands.

"Please don't ever do that again," I said, quietly. "Why did you?"

"I was jealous," he said. "After Emma hugged and kissed me, you both left and I was alone again."

"I've been jealous of you my whole life," I admitted. "You always see the best in people. I would hate to see you lose that ability."

"Maybe I've already lost it."

"You're not alone, Adam," I said, with tears in my eyes.

"That's how I feel."

"You're not alone," I repeated. "We've already lost our mum, but you didn't think about that."

"I think about her every day,'" Adam said, angrily.

"If you remember what it was like when Mum died, why did you want to leave me and Dad to go on without you?"

"I'm sorry," Adam said, staring at his hands.

"Adam. Look at me." I waited until he raised his head. "You're my brother and I love you very much. And I don't want to lose you."

"I mean that much to you?" Adam stared at

me as if he'd never seen me before.

"Don't be so stupid! Of course you do, you silly arse."

"Language!" Adam said with the smallest of smiles.

"It's not funny, Adam."

"I'm sorry," he said. "I won't do it again."

"Promise me."

"I promise." He smiled, but it was only when he wiped his hand across my face that I realised that I was crying.

"Don't you know that boys don't cry?" he asked.

"Boys don't cry, but real men do," I replied.

We hugged each other and it felt really, really good.

"I have to help make dinner now," I said. "Are you going to come downstairs?"

"I . . . maybe tomorrow."

"Definitely tomorrow. OK?"

"OK," Adam said.

Chapter Forty

The world outside my room

ADAM

After Dante left, I picked up Josh's letter. I didn't want to read it, but I didn't want to throw it away either – at least not yet. So I put it in my cupboard under some jumpers.

Yesterday, when Emma hugged me, was the first time that someone had touched me in months and I felt so alone. I missed my friends. I missed school. I missed my life. The world was happening outside my door and I wasn't a part of it. I missed my mum more than ever. In the past, if I was hurting, she would hug me until I felt better. But when she died, the hugging stopped.

I did a stupid, stupid thing.

I promised Dante that I'll never do that again,

and I mean it.

My room had kept me safe over the past few months, but now it felt too small. I looked at myself in the mirror. Yes, my right eye drooped and you could still see a couple of scars. But only a couple.

I opened my door and went downstairs. I could hear voices coming from the kitchen and the sound of Emma laughing. That was something else I'd missed all these months.

Taking a deep breath, I opened the door and entered the room.

"Hi, everybody," I smiled. "Do you mind if I join you?"

Chapter Forty-one

Together

DANTE

We all stared at Adam like he was a ghost. Emma was the first person to react.

"Unckey," she said, walking towards him and holding her arms up.

"How's my favourite niece?" he said, picking her up and smiling.

"How are you, son?" Dad asked, as Adam put Emma back down on her feet. "If you ever need someone to talk to," Dad told him, "I'll always be here for you."

Then suddenly, Dad hugged him. And after a second Adam hugged him back. I watched them with tears in my eyes.

"Me now," Emma said, holding her arms towards Adam and making us all laugh.

"Dinner's ready!" Aunt Jackie said.

As we sat down to eat, I watched my family. Right now, we were all happy. Before Emma arrived, we shared the same house, but that was all. But now we were a family, and we were together. And for now, that was all that mattered.

About Quick Reads

"Reading is such an important building block for success"
~ Jojo Moyes

Quick Reads are short books written
by best-selling authors.

Did you enjoy this Quick Read?

Tell us what you thought by filling in
our short survey. Scan the **QR code**
to go directly to the survey or
visit **bit.ly/QR2024**

Thanks to Penguin Random House and Hachette and to all
our publishing partners for their ongoing support.

A special thank you to Jojo Moyes for her generous donation in
2020-2022 which helped to build the future of Quick Reads.

Quick Reads is delivered by The Reading Agency, a UK charity
with a mission to get people fired up about reading, because
everything changes when you read.

www.readingagency.org.uk   @readingagency   #QuickReads

The Reading Agency Ltd. Registered number: 3904882 (England & Wales)
Registered charity number: 1085443 (England & Wales)
Registered Office: 24 Bedford Row, London, WC1R 4EH
The Reading Agency is supported using public funding by
Arts Council England.

Find your next Quick Read...

For 2024 we have selected 6 popular
Quick Reads for you to enjoy!

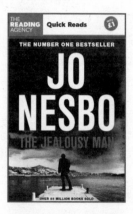

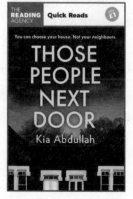

Quick Reads are available to buy in paperback or ebook and to borrow from your local library. For a complete list of titles and more information on the authors and their books visit **www.readingagency.org.uk/quickreads**

Continue your reading journey with The Reading Agency:

Reading Ahead

Challenge yourself to complete six reads by taking part in **Reading Ahead** at your local library, college or workplace: **readingahead.org.uk**

Reading
Groups
for Everyone

Join **Reading Groups for Everyone** to find a reading group and discover new books: **readinggroups.org.uk**

World Book Night

Celebrate reading on **World Book Night** every year on 23 April: **worldbooknight.org**

Summer Reading Challenge

Read with your family as part of the **Summer Reading Challenge: summerreadingchallenge.org.uk**

For more information on our work and the power of reading please visit our website: **readingagency.org.uk**

More from Quick Reads

If you enjoyed the 2024 Quick Reads
please explore our 6 titles from 2023.

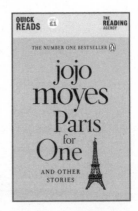

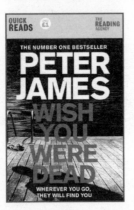

For a complete list of titles and more information
on the authors and their books visit:
www.readingagency.org.uk/quickreads

PENGUIN BOOKS

UK | USA | Canada | Ireland | Australia
India | New Zealand | South Africa

Penguin Books is part of the Penguin Random House group of companies
whose addresses can be found at global.penguinrandomhouse.com.
www.penguin.co.uk www.puffin.co.uk www.ladybird.co.uk

Boys Don't Cry first published by Doubleday Childrens 2010
Penguin Readers edition first published by Penguin Books Ltd 2022
This Quick Reads edition published 2024
001

Original text written by Oneta Malorie Blackman
Text for Penguin Readers edition adapted by Maeve Clarke
Original copyright © Oneta Malorie Blackman 2010
Text copyright © Penguin Books Ltd, 2022
Illustrated by Ana Latese
Illustrations copyright © Penguin Books Ltd, 2022

The moral right of the original author has been asserted

Printed and bound in Great Britain by Clays Ltd, Elcograf S.p.A.

The authorized representative in the EEA is Penguin Random House Ireland, Morrison Chambers,
32 Nassau Street, Dublin D02 YH68.

A CIP catalogue record for this book is available from the British Library

ISBN: 978-0-241-68810-6

All correspondence to:
Penguin Books
Penguin Random House Children's
One Embassy Gardens, 8 Viaduct Gardens,
London SW11 7BW